FOCUS
ON BRITISH COLUMBIA

FOCUS
ON BRITISH COLUMBIA

Text by Lyndon Grove
Photographs by British Columbians

WESTWORLD PUBLICATIONS LTD.
VANCOUVER

Westworld Publications Ltd.,
P.O. Box 6680,
Vancouver, British Columbia V6B 4L4
Canada

Canadian Cataloguing in Publication Data

Grove, Lyndon, 1932-
  Focus on British Columbia

  ISBN 0-9690807-0-0
  1. British Columbia - Description and travel -
1950 -   - Views.* 2. Roads - British Columbia -
History. I. Title.
FC3812.G76   917.11'044'0222   C81-091216-3
F1087.8.G76

Photo on page 2 of Pacific dogwood (*Cornus nuttallii*) by Sharon
Connaughty. Painting on page 6 by Bob Banks. Historical
photographs pages 8 through 19 courtesy Vancouver Public
Library, Historical Photographs Section.

Design and typesetting by Westworld Publications Ltd. Colour
separations by Cleland-Kent Ltd., Vancouver. Printed and
bound in Canada by Evergreen Press Ltd., Vancouver.

Preface

It has been seventy-five years since a small group of motorists banded together in Victoria to form B.C.'s first automobile club, the forerunner of today's British Columbia Automobile Association. Little did that group of "automobilists" realize that their tiny organization, founded initially for social fellowship, would spread across British Columbia until it had joined more than 360,000 motorists in a common bond.

Early in their history the amalgamating Vancouver Island and Lower Mainland auto clubs relinquished many of their social activities to get down to the real concerns of motoring — good roads, just laws and service to members. Ultimately all of British Columbia was to benefit from these aims; the growing popularity of the automobile early in this century made possible an unheard-of mobility and spurred the building and improvement of roads throughout our province.

To commemorate our 75th anniversary, we of the British Columbia Automobile Association have chosen to publish a pictorial representation of our province as captured by the cameras and imaginations of our members. We wish to give special thanks to the many talented amateur B.C. photographers whose contributions have made this book possible.

Much has changed over the past seventy-five years. Motorists are no longer the embattled minority they were when our automobile association was first formed. But many challenges remain and we will continue striving to ensure even greater benefits for members as the association looks ahead to its first century of service to British Columbians.

I have never seen anything like this country. It is so wild that I cannot find words to describe our situation. We had to pass where no human being should venture.
Simon Fraser, 1808

Driving through the Monashee Mountains in a midnight thunder storm, on a crumbling cliffside road just wide enough for your car, you begin to think that Simon Fraser was right. Especially when a flash of lightning illuminates a sign warning "Avalanche Area". But that sort of road is now a rarity in British Columbia. Between 1954 and 1979, almost three billion dollars was spent on B.C. highways. The province now has a network of 53,000 kilometres of roads, and the Ministry of Transportation and Highways has 10,000 employees at work from Fernie to Dease Lake.

Travelling east-west across the province is an engineering miracle. British Columbia is a topographical roller-coaster of mountain ranges (average height 2,400 metres) and canyons, scoring the land from north to south. Besides those obstacles to road-building, the province's 948,600 square kilometres are marked by dry belts and rain forests, hundreds of rivers and lakes, various soil and rock conditions, rainfalls up to 3,800 mm a year and snowfalls to 15,200 mm. "Within its borders," writes Raymond Baines in *Frontier to Freeway*, "[British Columbia presents] almost every engineering problem found in other parts of the world — and a few found nowhere else."

The first path-builders were Indians. Their trails set the pattern for many later roadways. Then came the fur traders of the Hudson's Bay Company and the North West Fur Trading Company. In the early 19th century they began carving trails west to the Pacific and east to the Northwest Territories. In 1853, Governor James Douglas assigned a committee to plan the province's first highway, from Victoria to Sooke. But it wasn't until the 1858 Fraser gold rush that anyone cared much about building roads into the mainland interior, the wild country that had been

known as New Caledonia.

In the spring of 1858, 30,000 gold seekers swarmed into the lower Fraser Valley. *The ways to this New Eldorado are several,* wrote William Carew Hazlitt. *There is, first, the route to the Isthmus of Panama. You leave Southampton on the 2nd of the month and reach Colon on the 25th. You get into the train, and, on arrival at its Pacific terminus, find a steamer which carries you on to San Francisco in about fourteen days. Thence steam wafts you on to the mouth of Frazer's River; and thence, again, the same power paddles you up to the realm of gold.*

There is another route by which the emigrant may reach British Columbia, through Canada and the United States, over the Rocky Mountains. Wagons can cross the Rocky Mountains at the Kootanie Pass. The autumn season is most favourable for this journey. But it must be clearly understood it will not do to take any luggage by this route. There appears to be on this line plenty of grass, water, timber and game, and security from Indian attacks.

Governor Douglas, seeing the arrival of the gold-diggers of 1858, moved first to secure the territory for the Crown and second to build roads to the gold fields. On August 2, royal assent was given to an act to provide government for British Columbia, where "divers of her Majesty's subjects and others. . . have resorted to and settled on certain wild and unoccupied territories on the North-west coast of North America. . ." Sir Edward Bulwer Lytton was exultant. "We are laying the foundations of what may become hereafter a magnificent abode for the human race," he declared. "We hope one day to connect the harbours of Vancouver with the Gulf of St. Lawrence."

Walter Moberly, a twenty-six-year-old Ontario engineer, had arrived in British Columbia that

One of the famous Cariboo Road camels.
DROMEDARY

year. A friend of the painter Paul Kane, he had enormous energy and imagination. He helped found Queensborough (later New Westminster); he searched for the "true northwest passage to the Pacific" and discovered Eagle Pass; and he had an idea for a transcontinental railway. Governor Douglas commissioned Moberly to study the feasibility of road-building into the Cariboo.

Meanwhile, miners were camped around Lillooet, and Douglas feared they might be cut off from supplies by winter snows. Ships could travel up the Fraser to Harrison, but a road was needed from there to Lillooet. To build it, Douglas enlisted five hundred miners who were sitting around Victoria, waiting for transportation to the gold fields. There was money up front, but it wasn't the government's. The governor (who was also Hudson's Bay Company factor) got the miners to post twenty-five dollars each as a "good

conduct" bond. The money was held by the company. When the men finished the road and arrived in Lillooet, they got their deposits back in supplies — provided, of course, by Hudson's Bay.

The Harrison-Douglas Road, as it was known, was completed in two months. The miners finished a serviceable wagon trail at the rate of six to ten kilometres a day. Then the first real road-builders arrived: the Royal Engineers, commanded by Colonel Richard Clement Moody. Moody looked at Moberly's studies of a route to the Cariboo and announced that he was ready to confront "those obstructive canyons of the Fraser."

The Royal Engineers (or Sappers) began work on the Cariboo Road in 1862. The path north was charted by Lieutenant R.C. Mayne of the Royal Navy, who had been attached to Moody's team, and Indian chief Captain St. Paul Loto. In charge of the work crews was Sergeant Jock McMurphy of Glasgow, a veteran of campaigns in Africa and

Freight wagons on the Cariboo Road.

9

the Crimea. Sergeant McMurphy looked something like George "Gabby" Hayes (Roy Rogers' sidekick) in a Royal Army uniform — white beard, querulous gaze, baggy trousers.

Work on the 640-kilometre road was troubled by smallpox, labour disputes and a monotonous diet. (Entry in Jock McMurphy's journal: "A case of brandy and a box of preserves for our gruel arrived, as we complained of having nothing to eat but beans and bacon three times a day, which is a very good thing now and then, but 21 times a week is too often.") But, within three years, the road was completed, and twenty-mule-team freight trains were packing supplies into the Cariboo.

The Cariboo Road, wrote Judge Howay, was "the pride of British Columbia, [a feat] of daring conception and skillful execution." The Sappers who worked on it were given ten percent of their wages in cash, ten percent in rations, and eighty percent in rural land around Queensborough.

Colonel Moody became Lieutenant-Governor and the province's first Chief Commissioner of Lands and Works.

Between the building of the Harrison-Douglas Road and the Cariboo Road, another important route was built through the south of the province. Governor Douglas assigned Moberly and another young engineer, Edgar Dewdney, to build a "mule road" between Hope and Vermilion Forks (now Princeton). Dewdney and Moberly built a 1.2 metre-wide corduroy road at a cost of $235 a kilometre. Eighty-five years later, the original Dewdney Trail became the Hope-Princeton Highway.

The Dewdney Trail was later extended to take prospectors to the 1864 gold rush at Wild Horse Creek in the East Kootenays. Governor Seymour ordered Dewdney to locate and construct a road through the mountains in one year and to do it for $50,000. Dewdney found a way to cross three ranges of the Monashees and Selkirks. He overran the cost

The bridge across Hagwilet Canyon built by the Gitksan Indians using abandoned telegraph cable.

10

B.C. Express Company's Stage Leaving Ashcroft for Cariboo 1889

by fifty percent, but he finished the 640-kilometre road within the deadline. The Dewdney Trail became the basis of most of Highway 3. Dewdney, not surprisingly, is a heroic figure to highway builders: He is commemorated by a bronze sculpture in the Transportation and Highways offices in Victoria. The engineer later became a member of the House of Commons, Indian Commissioner in the Northwest Territories and Lieutenant-Governor of B.C.

The mules trudging up the Cariboo Road could carry packs as heavy as 180 kilograms. But a camel, two pioneer entrepreneurs discovered, could carry 270 kilograms. John C. Callbreath (ominous name, as it turned out) saw an advertisement placed by the U.S. Army. The transport service had been employing camels in Texas, but now wanted to sell them. Frank Laumeister set off for San Francisco to make a deal for two dozen used camels. ("How many miles this beast got on 'er?") He bought them for $300 each.

The camels were shipped to Victoria by boat.

Standing on display at Douglas and Johnson Streets, two of the beasts were offended by the prodding of a lout. They chased him off, and then, sensing freedom, made for Cadboro Bay. The rest of the herd was manoeuvred to the Cariboo. On August 20, 1862, the first camel pack train stalked into Lightning Creek.

But the experiment was not a success. The rough terrain tore the camels' feet, and others perished in the winter snows. Worst of all was the camels' ineffable halitosis, enough to cause chaos among the other pack-train animals. Horses and mules would stampede to get away. The cause of this desert breath may have been the camels' diet: They liked to eat the miners' laundry, the grubbier the better. Harry Guillod wrote in his diary that the humped beasts "had a neat way of walking over your tent and eating your shirts."

The camels were released to roam the Cariboo. Some became ranch pets. Others ended up as ranch

A B.C. Express stagecoach at Ashcroft in 1889.

stew. But some lived off the land for another forty years. In September, 1980, Lillooet dedicated "The Bridge of the 23 Camels" to the animals. And that year's December issue of the *Lillooet District Historical Society Bulletin* saluted "all the birds and beasts that are traditionally associated with Christmas, turkeys and doves, donkeys and camels. Merry Christmas to all, especially camels."

British Columbia's first Road Act was introduced in 1860 "to provide for the repair, improvement and regulation of roads on Vancouver Island and its dependencies." Every resident of the district was required to spend six days a year working on the roads. The alternative: a tax of six shillings, threepence.

Between 1871 and 1880 as much as 44.48% of the province's revenue was spent on roads and bridges. Many settlers depended on road building as a primary source of employment. But even with all this activity, R.E. Gosnell wrote in the 1897 *British Columbia Digest of Reliable Information* that "many fertile sections are yet practically isolated and accessible still only by cayuse over pack trails, canoes, boats or small steamers and along wagon roads."

Ferries had been in use since 1859, when a barge was hauled across the Fraser at Yale. There were no ferry schedules and sometimes passengers would wait hours for the ferryman to turn up. And sometimes he didn't turn up. In 1864, the ferry operator on the Homathko River was killed by Indians.

Cariboo rancher Shorty Schrader ran an aerial ferry over the canyon at Big Bar, forty miles north of Lillooet. Anglican Bishop Acton Sillitoe crossed the canyon in a basket to make parish calls. He and his wife also travelled up the railway line (the Canadian Pacific crews had arrived in 1880) pumping a handcar. The trains didn't follow regular schedules, either, and the Sillitoes often had to leap off the tracks.

Stage coaches rumbled over the province's roads. Bill Ballou's Pioneer Fraser River Express was the first, up from San Francisco. Best known of the B.C. stagecoach services was BX Stage Lines, operated by Francis Barnard. Barnard's principal driver was Steve Tingley, later known as the "pioneer whip of the Cariboo Road." Tingley became sole owner of the B.C. Express, a Barnard offshoot, and married a daughter of Frank Laumeister, the camel caravan man. One of the most popular stage stops in the territory was Loch Lomond at 74 Mile House, established by Jock McMurphy after he turned in his sergeant's stripes.

The C.P.R. established its Inland Lake and River Service, and huge sternwheelers moved ponderously through the waters. The last of these, the S.S. *Moyie*, was retired in 1957 after fifty-nine years on Kootenay Lake. Bought by the Kootenay Lake Historical Society for one dollar, it's now a museum in Kaslo. In the summer of 1894, the Fraser River was in full flood, and the Rev. John A. Logan described the paddlewheeler *Courser* "nervously threading its way through fields and over fences, avoiding obstacles of all kinds — buildings, poles, logs, stumps — [making] a call at the Harrison Hotel, tying up to a barn at the back."

With all those canyons and waterways, the province has had to have a lot of bridges. By 1980, there were more than 3,000. One of the first was built at Hagwilget Canyon by Gitksan Indians. They recycled miles of telegraph wire left behind by the engineer Colonel Bulkley. Bulkley had hoped to build an overland telegraph line to Europe, crossing over the Aleutians and Siberia from northern B.C. When someone else beat him to it with a trans-Atlantic cable, Bulkley abandoned the wire and moved on. The 'Ksan strung poles together with the wire and hung a bridge over a forty-five-metre span between thirty-metre cliffs. The bridge was used for half a century.

J.W. Trutch asked not for whom the bridge tolls — it tolled for him. Trutch built the Alexandra Suspension Bridge in 1863. The government didn't have any money for him, but they allowed him to

collect toll fares for seven years. Impressed by Trutch's acumen, the government made him Commissioner of Lands and Works. Another bridge-builder/toll-collector was Thomas Spence, whose name has ever since remained as firmly linked to Bridge as Stanfield's is to underwear.

In 1899, Lands and Works sent out men on bicycles to measure the miles of completed roadways in the province. The cyclometers registered 5,615.5 miles (9,037 km) of roads and 4,414.5 miles (7,104 km) of trails. Highway building in British Columbia was forty years old.

"By wire Victoria is only a second from Nelson, but by automobile it is impossible." So complained a Kootenay resident in 1906. The age of the automobile was about to begin in British Columbia, and the focus of highway construction would change. Roads, once built for fur traders, gold miners and settlers, would from now on

be built for automobiles. And, with the advent of the automobile, road-building mushroomed: It was the car that created the need for most roads in B.C.

The Good Roads Association, formed in 1900, had begun a twenty-five-year campaign for improved highways, and the province had introduced, in 1904, its first tax on gasoline and its first motor vehicle licence fee: $36 a year. Roads were built using Mexican asphalt, wood blocks (tarred and untarred), bricks and concrete. By 1918, there were 24,000 kilometres of roads criss-crossing British Columbia.

Motor touring was a new leisure fashion. Miss E.H. Grant described "A Motor Trip on Vancouver Island, B.C." for the January, 1915 issue of the *British Columbia Motorist*, journal of the Vancouver Auto Club:

Early Saturday morning we started for the Malahat Drive and Shawnigan Lake. The ride up was lovely and without mishap. Our course was up Government Street, out past the Gorge, where

A group of men in Vancouver's first automobile.

Friday we had tea in the famous Japanese Tea Gardens; then along the Island Highway, a splendid road. The Malahat Drive is dreaded by a few nervous people, mostly women, but there is no cause for fear — the road is excellent, and although narrow with sharp turns, with ordinary care and a dependable machine one can make good time. The road climbs to a height of more than twenty-five hundred feet, and the view across the Saanich Inlet is a beautiful one. The mountains tower above on the left, and on the right are the green tops of the tall trees, with the blue waters below. Across in the distance is Saanich peninsula with its green fields and well-kept homesteads. We climbed but to descend again. The whole descent is like a dream to me, so rapidly was it accomplished.

The automobile had become an important factor in the life of British Columbia, with social, economic and political ramifications. In 1915, T.S. Baxter placed this advertisement in the *British Columbia Motorist*: "To the Motorists of Vancouver: In soliciting your vote and influence for re-election as Mayor, I would state that during my term of office I have endeavoured and succeeded in bringing about harmonious feelings between the Motorists of the City and the police." In the same desire for harmony, the magazine printed this helpful advice: "Don't violate the provisions of the Motor Act. The officer who serves you with the summons does not like the job."

In 1920 (the year B.C. motorists moved to the right side of the road, as instructed by the new Highways Act) there were 28,000 motor vehicles registered in the province. By 1930, there were 98,938. As early as 1928, there were drivers demanding a cross-country highway. *Western Canadian Motorist* exclaimed, "The Trans-Canada Highway! Every Motorist should agitate to bring this once impossible dream into the realms of realization." The magazine even had the route through the Rockies picked: Calgary to Banff to Golden to Revelstoke. That same year the *Motorist* carried this account:

William Ball, an employee of the New Westminster firm of T.J. Trapp Ltd., accompanied by G.T. Brooks of the Kelly Douglas sales staff, established a new record by travelling to California and back in little more than two days. They started in a Chevrolet Imperial landau sedan from New Westminster at 8:06 p.m., being officially checked by the Canadian National Telegraph office. At Yreka, Cal., the first telegraph office within the boundary of California, their credentials were certified to by the operator at 10:50 p.m. the following day. The time of their return to New Westminster was vouched for by the Great Northern Railway telegraph office at 12:28 a.m., two days later. Thus the return trip was made in 52 hours and 22 minutes. The distance travelled was 1,536 miles, an average speed of 30 miles per hour was maintained, and an average of 35 miles per gallon of gasoline was secured. The oil consumption was one quart.

Tourist — "I say, old man, is this the road to Pickle Centre?"

Old Inhabitant — "Wal, yes, it's the road, all right — but you better turn around if you want to get there."

Autoist — "I haven't paid a cent for repairs on my machine all the ten months I have had it."

Friend — "So the man who did the repairs told me."

Mr. Spendix — "Any instalments due today?"

Mrs. Spendix — "No, dear. I think not."

Mr. S. — "Any payments due on the house, the radio, the furniture, the rugs or the books?"

Mrs. S. — "No."

Mr. S. — "Then I have ten dollars we don't need. What do you say we buy a new car?"

The largest highway project of the pre-war years was the building of a link between B.C. and the Prairies. A narrow **gravel** road was shaped beside the winding Columbia River. This Big Bend route was scary enough to instantly whiten the hair of a

motorist from Moose Jaw, especially if he encountered a bus coming toward him on the slim canyon ledge. He would then have to back up, often around corners, until he found a recessed passing place in the mountainside. No wonder most drivers going to and from the Prairies preferred to detour through the United States.

Through the 1930s depression and World War II there was little road construction and few cars were sold. The one major road-building task was the development of the Alaska Highway. After Japan and the United States went to war in 1941, it was feared that Japan might seize Alaska and use the west coast as an invasion route. The Alaska Highway, connecting Fairbanks and Dawson Creek, was built as an alternate route for U.S. military transport.

In 1945, B.C. road-builders got started again. The province's Department of Public Works borrowed $10 million for road construction. The next year, the cost was $18 million. Minister of Public Works between 1945 and 1952 was E.C. Carson. Under his administration were built the Pine Point (John Hart) Highway, joining Prince George and Dawson Creek; and the Hope-Princeton Highway, the first modern route between the interior and the coast.

Roadside plaque on the Bella Coola Road: *At this site on September 26th, 1953, two bulldozers operated by Alf Bracewell and George Delshaug touched blades to symbolize the opening of a road through the mountain barrier of the Coast Range marked out by Elijah Gurr. Two years of strenuous local effort thus established a third highway route across this province to the Pacific Ocean, through an area originally explored by Lieutenant H. Spencer Palmer, R.E., 1862.*

For the first time, all of the province's far-flung communities were being connected by road. Prosperity had finally come, and the sound of the road-grader was heard through the land. Not everyone was pleased. Richmond P. Hobson, Jr., in an essay called "Bulldozers At My Heels," complained that "inch by inch, mile by mile, road contractors have pushed me northwards."

"Most people want roads," wrote Hobson. "They want good ones. They petition parliament, plead before provincial legislatures, get down on their knees before Public Works Commissions. I hate good roads." But he realized there was no stopping the road-builders. "If I start with a bunch of pack-horses and an axe, and find some quiet sheltered spot on the tundra where I can raise reindeer, a road will soon follow." Hobson's one plaintive request: "Don't pave a path to my door."

In 1954, highways projects of Public Works were put into a new department, the Department of Highways. The minister in charge was Philip A. Gaglardi, a cherubic radio evangelist from Kamloops. Gaglardi was in command from 1952 until 1968, an epic period of road-building. For seventeen years, the most-seen road sign in B.C. was "Sorry for the inconvenience. P.A. Gaglardi."

In those years, the province extended the Island Highway to Kelsey Bay, completed Southern Trans-Provincial Highway 3, connected B.C. to northern Alberta with links from Highways 5 and 16 to the Yellowhead and built the last of seven tunnels (90 to 600 metres long) on the old Cariboo Road route through the Fraser Canyon. The Lions Gate Bridge was bought from the Guinness interests for $6 million, the cost of building the bridge from Vancouver to the North Shore in 1938. A 720-metre floating bridge was built on Okanagan Lake, and the Vancouver-Blaine Freeway including the Deas (now Massey) Tunnel was finished. A three-kilometre section of the Hope-Princeton Highway had to be rebuilt after a 1965 landslide down Johnson Mountain filled the Nicolum Creek Valley with ninety million tonnes of rock, mud, snow and trees.

In 1962, the province's most spectacular highway was opened through the Rogers Pass. It was the trans-Canada route the *Western Canadian Motorist* had called for in 1928: from Golden to Revelstoke. The Rogers Pass route meant no more white-

Motor-car on a Vancouver Island highway circa 1912.

A 1930 car passing through a narrow tunnel on the Cariboo Highway.

knuckle drives along the Big Bend, and traffic between the Prairies and British Columbia immediately increased a thousand percent. In 1980, 1.4 million vehicles entered B.C. via Rogers Pass.

In 1964, the last section of the Trans-Canada Highway was put into place with the erection of the Port Mann Bridge across the Fraser — the world's longest (2,100 metres) high-level, stiffened, tied-arch, orthotropic plate-deck bridge.

In July, 1958, a seamen's strike stopped marine traffic between Vancouver Island and the B.C. mainland. The idea of a government-operated ferry system was presented, but, initially, the government approached private companies. It would build highway and wharf facilities if private business would provide the ferries. When there were no takers for

this offer, the Highways Department went into the ferry business. Its first two vessels were the M.V. *Sidney* (now *Queen of Sidney*) and M.V. *Tsawwassen* (now *Queen of Tsawwassen*). The ferries made their first crossings in the summer of 1960. By 1980 the British Columbia Ferry Corporation was running a fleet of more than fifty ferries, connecting the mainland and Vancouver Island between Tsawwassen (Vancouver) and Swartz Bay (Victoria); Horseshoe Bay (Vancouver) and Nanaimo; and Kelsey Bay and Prince Rupert (a 530-kilometre journey). Also served were the Gulf Islands in the Strait of Georgia.

Between 1964 and 1974, the province's population rose thirty-seven percent, from 1,745,000 to 2,395,000. But the four-wheeled population grew by

sixty-six percent. Motor vehicle registrations increased from 705,000 to 1,171,000. By 1979, there had been another rise of twenty-seven percent. B.C. has always had the highest ratio of passenger cars per capita in Canada. In 1979, there was one motor vehicle registered for every 1.8 persons.

Highways costs have increased, as well. The province's record 1946-47 budget for roads, $18 million, would buy only thirty-two kilometres of four-lane highway in the late 1970s. The 1979 budget of the (once again re-named) Ministry of Transportation and Highways was more than $440 million, twelve times the total budget for all provincial government departments in 1946.

As British Columbia accelerated into the eighties, highways projects included the connection of High-

way 16 at Kitwanga with the Alaska Highway at Watson Lake, a new route through Coquihalla Pass joining Hope and Merritt, reconstruction of Highway 23 between Revelstoke and Mica Creek, reconstruction of Highway 16 between Terrace and Prince Rupert, and upgrading of sections of the Hart Highway on Route 97.

One hundred and twenty-one years after the passing of British Columbia's first Road Act, the province's 50,000 kilometres of roadways, many of them multi-lane highways, were lined, often bumper to bumper, with automobiles, motor homes, campers, tour buses, motorbikes, transport trucks, ten-speed bicycles, and hitchhikers. Simon Fraser would be astonished. Nobody thumbed a ride when he came down the canyon.

Construction of the Port Mann Bridge.

19

Top: *Yellow arnica in Manning Park.*
Photo Gayle Russell

Right: *Bighorn sheep, Crater Mountain.*
Photo Jim Moody

Previous page: *Chesterman Beach,*
Tofino. Photo Pat O'Rourke

Top: *Old ranch house, Osoyoos area.*
Photo John F. Moore

Left: *Farrier at work. Photo Sven Buemann*

Top: *Vancouver skyline at night. Photo*
Marin Petkov

Right: Seagull with young, Departure Bay
Terminal. Photo Randy Aitken

Previous page: Gulf Islands sunset. Photo Dorothea Clarke

Left: Sunset, Summit Lake. Photo Beverley Dockrill

Bottom: Western columbine **(Aquilegia formosa)**. Photo Brandon Cheshire

Page 32: Nitobe Gardens, University of British Columbia. Photo David Lin

Page 33: Lion Dance, Chinese New Year, Vancouver. Photo Jean Begg

Right: *Cates Park, North Vancouver. Photo Frank Mayrs*

Top: Winter ascent, Yoho National Park.
Photo Alan Dibb

Top: *Gulls on Okanagan Lake. Photo Jerald Walliser*

Right: *Polar bears, Stanley Park. Photo Myrtle James*

Page 38: Sunset, Stanley Park. Photo Ron Stanaitis

Page 39: Bridal Veil Falls. Photo David Greenberg

Top: Bald eagle. Photo A. Kelly

Above: Raccoon in tree, Victoria. Photo W.G. McIntosh

Right: Totem pole, Queen Charlotte Islands. Photo Erich Hoyt

Left: Capilano Dam. Photo Catherine Bishop

Bottom: *Grasses, near Signal Hill, Pacific Rim National Park. Photo Hilda MacLeod*

Above: *Children on Combers Beach, north of Ucluelet. Photo Dr. J. Raymond*

Previous page: *Peace Valley, east of Kelowna. Photo H. Agar*

Top: *Starfish* **(Solaster stimpsoni)**
Victoria. Photo Stephen Mitchell

Left: *Seagull, Lillooet Lake. Photo Rudolf
Lenhart*

Left: Fishing boats in Rivers Inlet. Photo Wayne and Francine Fisher

Top: Cross-country skiing in the Cariboo.
Photo Gail Ross

Right: Doe and fawns, Manning Park.
Photo Steven Short

50

Left: Hoar-frost on holly leaves. Photo
Sharon Connaughty

Previous page: Boats in Vancouver
harbour. Photo Mark Kusic

Right: *Sailboats in winter. Photo R.
Todhunter*

Bottom: *Snow on berries, Stanley Park.
Photo Marin Petkov*

Page 56: Cathedral Provincial Park. Photo G.W. McCahon

Page 57: Capilano Canyon. Photo D. Ling

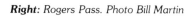

Right: Rogers Pass. Photo Bill Martin

Bottom: Prickly pear cactus *(Opuntia polyacantha)* in flower. Photo Barb Clemes

Above: *Girl pumping water, Kootenays.*
Photo Dan Clarke

Above: Tulips in Stanley Park. Photo Marin Petkov

Left: Yellow **Parnassius clodius** at work. Photo Brandon Cheshire

Above: *Black Tusk in winter. Photo Steven Short*

Above: *Spring in Queen Elizabeth Park.*
Photo R. Albert

Above: *Painted Bluffs. Photo Dixie Edmiston*

Left: *Man with antique threshing machine. Photo D. Thayer*

Top: Fly agaric *(**Amanita muscaria**).*
Photo Stephen Mitchell

Bottom: Dwarf dogwood *(**Cornus**
canadensis). Photo Beverley Dockrill*

Previous page: *Fishing on Howe Sound.*
Photo Brian Blackwell

Right: *Bridal Veil Falls. Photo Douglas*
Buchan

68

Top: Entrance Island lighthouse, Gabriola.
Photo N. Mitchell

*Right: Starfish **(Pisaster ochraceus)**, Mayne Island. Photo Sheena McDonald*

Top: *False Creek marina, Vancouver.*
Photo Douglas Buchan

Left: *Blue heron* **(Ardea herodias)**. *Photo*
Robert Panting

Previous page: Killer whales on the move. Photo Erich Hoyt

Right: Loggers' carnival. Photo W.G. Grant

Bottom: Faces of British Columbia. Photo Roy Londry

Left: Boom boat round-up. Photo W.G. Grant

Bottom: *Red leg frog, Nelson Island. Photo J.D. Manley*

Above: *Rocky shore, Tent Island. Photo*
Dan Clarke

Above: *Lions Gate Bridge. Photo Ron Stanaitis*

Above: *Fir forest. Photo Dr. Marion Rogers*

Above: *Silver-weed (**Potentilla pacifica**).*
Photo Clive Bryson

Previous page: Miners Bay, Mayne Island.
Photo Sheree Liversidge

Right: *The Gang Ranch. Photo Sven Buemann*

Bottom: *Mountain laurel (**Kalmia polifolia**). Photo Jan Raymond*

Left: Twin-flowers **(Linnaea borealis)**.
Photo Beverley Dockrill

Left: The ubiquitous squirrel. Photo Lois
Hornstra

Left: Hole-in-the-Ice Pole, Kitwancool,
near Hazelton. Photo Fred Waldburg

Above: Sunset, Spanish Banks,
Vancouver. Photo Judith Jardine

Page 90: Low tide, Savary Island. Photo
E. Patrick

Page 91: Grouse on headframe of old mine,
Nickel Plate Mountain. Photo Jim Moody

Right: Boundary Bay at low tide. Photo
John Black

Left: Fisherman on Bob Quinn Lake.
Photo Fred Waldburg

Above: *Vancouver in snow. Photo M.O. Bulling*

Page 100: *St. Saviour's Anglican Church, Barkerville. Photo Betty Archer*

Page 101: *Cape Scott shoreline. Photo G. McCahon*

Above: *South ridge fissure, Singing Pass.
Photo Jay W. Page*

Left: *Thistles* **(Cirsium vulgare)**. *Photo
Peter S. Heaster*

Above: *Tow-headed babies (seedheads of* **Anemone occidentalis**). *Photo Jim Moody*

Above: *Canoeing on Matheson Lake,*
Vancouver Island. Photo Rudolf Lenhart

Above: *Seiner in Johnstone Strait. Photo Erich Hoyt*

Right: *Mount Alfred. Photo Tony Mathews*

Previous page: *Surf fishing at McKenzie Cove. Photo Pat O'Rourke*

Above: Knutsford. Photo J. Budge

Left: Sea grass and driftwood, Oyster Bay.
Photo L. McLaughlin

Previous page: Seagull in flight. Photo
Wayne and Francine Fisher

Page 114: *Mushrooms and fungus. Photo Carol MacMillan*

Page 115: *Sunset, Long Beach. Photo J. McAdam*

Left: *North Shore mountains in winter. Photo Vlado Matisic*

Below: *Beardtongue* **(Penstemon davidsonii)***. Photo Jan Raymond*

Page 118: Long Beach. Photo Dan Clarke

Page 119: Alpine glacier, Mount Matier (Lillooet area). Photo Margaret Glimhagen

Previous page: Snow scene, Hart Highway. Photo David Greenberg

Below: Government Wharf, Tofino. Photo Dr. J. Raymond

Right: Swan in Lost Lagoon. Photo Mark Kusic

Right: Vancouver skyline after snowfall.
Photo Vlado Matisic

Top: *Old schoolhouse, Fort Steele. Photo Jacqueline McGarrigle*

Bottom: *Spoolmak Days rodeo, Kamloops. Photo J. Budge*

Above: *Cathedral Grove, Vancouver Island. Photo Lorne Zarazun*

Top: *Cattle round-up, west of Williams Lake. Photo Beverley Dockrill*

Right: *Skunk cabbage* **(Lysichitum americanum)**, *Ucluelet. Photo Hilda MacLeod*

Left: Trees in Farewell Canyon. Photo M.
Chambers

Above: *Country road near Dawson Creek.*
Photo G.R. Clare

Left: *Fishing boats in Active Pass. Photo*
Jerald Walliser

Top: *Ships in English Bay. Photo David Newell*

Right: *Clown blowing bubbles, Granville Island, Vancouver. Photo R. Todhunter*

Previous page: *Pictographs, Mara Lake. Photo S.B. Perry*

Left: *Windsurfers on English Bay. Photo Frank Mayrs*

Next page: *Lake O'Hara area. Photo Jill MacDonald*

Above: *Sea Festival fireworks, Vancouver.*
Photo Vivienne Lenhart